CHEF

—— BY ——

STEP ®

Chef by Step
For the Beginner Chef Volume 1

Published By Chef Laurie LLC

Recipes by Laurie Erickson
www.ChefLaurie.com

All Images and designs by Jake Morrill
www.Morrillustrations.com

Printed in the United Sates by Book Masters, INC

ISBN -10: 0-615-27844-2
ISBN- 13: 978-615-27844-5

The Chef by Step series is dedicated to all of the frustrated people wanting to learn how to cook, and need recipes that they can easily follow.

To all of the busy Moms out there who need basic, easy, economical, nutritious meals for their families that even their children can prepare.

Author

First and foremost I must thank grown children Bonnie Maya and Jake, Whom are my biggest Inspiration.
Without them I never would have created so many recipes

To My Husband Joel for his incredible support

To all of my Students over the last 25 years for begging me to finally write a cookbook.

My great friend Artie Richards who is living proof that learning how to cook can change your life

Artist

To my loving parents, you are the reason I run fast

To every beautiful thing that inspires artists to chase their dream

INTRODUCTION

We hear it every day. *"Eat more vegetables." "Eat less fat." "Eat more whole grains."* We are inundated with information saying certain foods are so good for us – The "power" foods, foods to slow the aging process, foods to prevent cancer. There's an abundance of information about WHY we need to eat better, but there's one giant obstacle ...   HOW?

My primary goal in life has been to teach people how to prepare nutritious, tasty meals for themselves and to encourage people to stop eating pre-packaged, processed foods.

I know that virtually no one is going to open a random cookbook, purchase the ingredients and follow a recipe. That scenario is very rare. Most people cook what they know how to cook, typically the same recipes over and over. These recipes are safe - they pretty much taste the same every time and they know their family will eat it.

Many people lack the confidence to prepare something new. And believe it or not - cooking is 80% confidence. Most people say *"I hate to cook!"*, when actually they are saying

"I don't know how to cook."
Hence my challenge.

If you were to consider preparing a new recipe for your family, you would want it to follow some strict rules. It would have:

Only a few ingredients
Not too many steps
No fancy ingredients
A reasonable cost
Not too many dishes to clean
Great taste and health benefits for you and your family

This is the inspiration for the Chef by Step® series. You will find that all of the recipes follow these criteria.

This first volume is geared toward the young or beginner chef. The recipes in this volume have very little chopping and utilize chopped frozen vegetables, which are actually sometimes better than fresh!

The upcoming volumes will be geared toward a specific group of people - The Bachelor. The College Student. The New Bride (or Groom). Then I will continue with Chef by Step® Desserts, Soups, Grilling, Vegetarian Options and more.

I thank you for purchasing this book and I hope it will allow you to change your life.

Chef Laurie

Contents

1 tablespoon (tbsp) = 3 teaspoons (tsp) = 15-20g

1/4 cup = 4 tablespoons

1/2 cup = 8 tablespoons

1 cup = 8 fluid ounces (fl oz)

2 cups = 1 pint (liquids)

2 pints (pt) = 1 quart

4 quarts = 1 gallon (gal)

16 ounces (oz) = 1 pound (lb)

SAFETY TIPS

* When cutting with a sharp knife, be sure to keep your fingers bent under.

* Make sure the handles from your pots and pans are never hanging over the edge of the stove

* Use a wooden spoon to stir things on the stove, it won't get hot like a metal spoon.

* If something on the stove catches fire, turn off the heat and cover the pot or pan with a tight fitting lid.

* If you spill something, clean it up right away or you may slip on it later.

* Always wear oven mitts when removing items from the microwave.

* When handling meat of any kind always wear rubber gloves.

* Always keep a fire extinguisher handy.

ALSO...

* Never leave the kitchen while something is on the stove

* Pull your hair back when cooking

Before You Start Cooking ...

Throughout this book you will often see this spray bottle being used. It's a great alternative to chemically processed sprays in a can. Just fill this food grade plastic bottle with olive oil and spray! Use it every time you need a little oil. These bottles are available at *ChefbyStep*.com

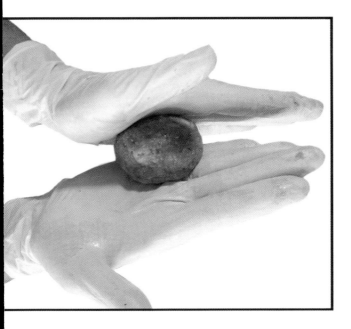

It's a good idea to wear rubber gloves when handling raw meat or fish. Simply throw them away after each use to prevent cross-contamination. These gloves can be found in the first aid section of most stores.

CHICKEN FAJITAS

With Whole Wheat Tortillas, Cheese, Peppers, and Onions

Cookie Sheet

Parchment Paper

Tongs

Knife

Cutting Board

1 Bag of Peppers and Onions
(12 oz)

Salsa

Whole Wheat
Tortillas

Cajun Seasoning

2 Cups Grated
Low Fat Cheese

2
Boneless
Chicken Breasts (4 oz each)

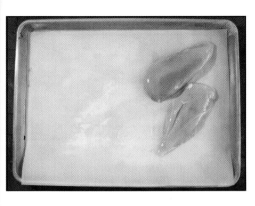

Preheat Oven to 425°.
Lay a piece of parchment paper
on cookie sheet.
Place chicken breasts on cookie sheet.

Sprinkle chicken with
cajun seasoning.

Place peppers and onions
on cookie sheet.

Place into oven.
Set timer for 15 minutes.

Remove from oven.

Place chicken onto cutting board.
Slice into strips.

Add desired amount of peppers,
onions, cheese, and salsa
to the tortillas.

TURKEY BURGERS

With Parmesan Polenta Fries

Rubber Gloves

Oven Mitts

Cookie Sheet

Parchment Paper

Parchment Paper

Knife

Ketchup

2 Whole Wheat Buns

Lettuce

8 oz Ground Turkey

Salt & Pepper

1/4 Cup Parmesan Cheese

1/2 Pound Cooked Polenta

" Polenta is ground and cooked corn, It's found in the produce section of most supermarkets "

Preheat oven to 450°
Lay a piece of parchment on a
cookie sheet.

Form turkey into flat hamburger shapes.

Place burgers on parchment paper.

Sprinkle with salt and pepper.

Slice polents into sticks,
place onto cookie sheet.

Sprinkle polenta with parmesan cheese.

Place into oven.
Bake for 15 minutes, and serve.

CHICKEN THIGHS

With Roasted Carrots, Green Beans, And Red Potatoes

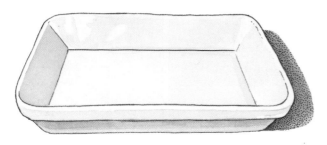

Roasting Pan

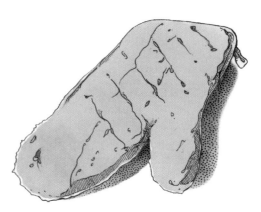

Oven Mitts

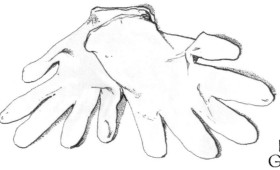

Rubber Gloves

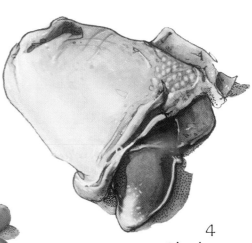

4 Chicken Thighs

8 to 12 Red Potatoes

8 to 12 Baby Carrots

Cajun Seasoning

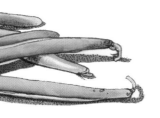

8 oz Green Beans

Preheat oven to 375°.
Put on rubber gloves.
Place chicken into pan.

Add red potatoes...

and carrots.

Sprinkle with cajun seasoning.

Place into oven.
Set timer for 40 minutes.

Snap ends off of green beans.

Carefully remove pan.
Add green beans.
Place into oven, set timer
for another 10 minutes.
And serve.

TOSTADAS

With Re-Fried Beans, Cheese, And Salsa

Cookie Sheet

Can Opener

Parchment Paper

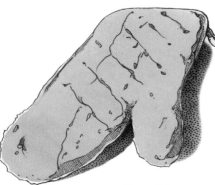
Oven Mitt

1 Cup grated low fat Cheese

Olive Oil

1/2 Cup Chopped Frozen Onions

4 Corn Tortillas

1/2 Cup Salsa

1 Can Refried Beans

2 Cups Shredded Lettuce

 CHEF LAURIE TIP | " On the re-fried beans ingredients list, make sure there is no lard or preservatives. "

Preheat oven to 425°.
Line a cookie sheet
with parchment paper.
Place tortillas on sheet.

Lightly spray tortillas
with olive oil.

Place in oven for 5 minutes.

Open can
of refried beans.

Remove tortillas from the oven.

Spread each tortilla with
1/2 cup of refried beans.

Sprinkle chopped onions
on top of beans.

Sprinkle with cheese.
Return pan to the oven and
bake for 5 minutes.

Top with salsa and lettuce.
And serve.

PITA PIZZA

With Chicken Sausage And Ceaser Salad

Cookie Sheet

Parchment Paper

Oven Mitt

Knife

Mixing Bowl

Spatula

1/2 Cup Marinara Sauce

1/4 Cup Dressing

1 Cup Shredded Monterey Jack Cheese

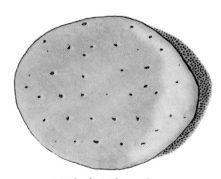

2 Whole Wheat Pitas

1 Package Chicken Sausage

4 Cups Chopped Romaine Lettuce

CHEF LAURIE TIP | " For a quick lunch, rap an extra pita in aluminum foil, peal back the foil and pop it into the toaster oven. "

Preheat oven to 425°.
Line a cookie sheet with
parchment paper.
Place pitas on paper.

Spread a thin layer of
marinara sauce on each pita.

Sprinkle with cheese.

Cut sausage into chunks.

Sprinkle sausage on top
of cheese.
Place into oven.
Set timer for 10 minutes.

Place 4 cups of lettuce into
mixing bowl.
Add 1/4 cup caesar salad
dressing.

Remove cookie sheet from oven.

Carefully place pizza on
cutting board.

Cut each pizza into 4 pieces,
And serve.

TORTELLINI SOUP

With Diced Tomatoes And Parmesan Cheese

Sauce Pan

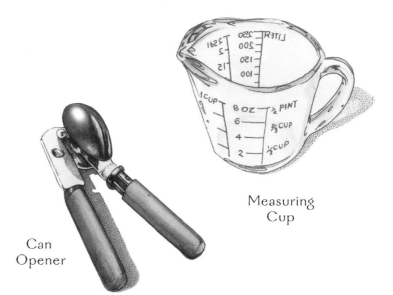

Can Opener

Measuring Cup

1/2 Cup Parmesan Cheese

1/2 Cup Frozen Peas

4 Cups Chicken Broth

1/2 Cup Diced Tomatoes

12 oz Tortellini

CHEF LAURIE TIP

" Fresh whole-wheat tortellini can be found in the refrigerated section of your local supermarket."

In a saucepan add chicken broth.
Set stove to high.

Bring to a boil.

Add tortellini.

Open can of tomatoes.

Add frozen peas...

canned tomatoes...

and grated parmesan cheese.
Stir contents.
Let simmer for 2 minutes.
And serve.

FISH TACOS

With Shredded Carrots And Fresh Salsa

Parchment Paper

Cookie Sheet

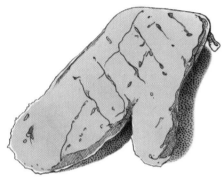

Oven Mitt

Rubber Gloves

2 Tablespoons
Cajun Seasoning

4 Taco Shells

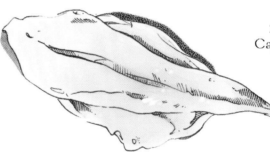

1/2 Pound Flounder filets

1 Cup Shredded Carrots

1 cup Salsa

1/2 cup Sour Cream

CHEF LAURIE TIP

"Always give your fish a smell before you buy it. It should not smell fishy. If it smells like bleach, drop it and run!."

Preheat oven to 425°.
Line a cookie sheet with
parchment paper.

Put on rubber gloves.
Place fish filets on
parchment paper.

Sprinkle fish filets with
cajun seasoning.

Place into oven.
Set timer for 8 minutes.

Remove fish from oven.
Carefully break fish up
into small chunks.

Fill taco shells with
desired amount of Fish...

Salsa...

Carrots...

and sour cream.
And serve.

PORK CHOPS

With Orange/Cranberry Sauce And Parmesan Spinach

Baking Dish

Can Opener

Measuring Cup

Sauce Pan

Tongs

Oven Mitts

Rubber Gloves

Measuring Spoons

15 oz Container fresh Baby Spinach

BABY SPINACH

4 Boneless Pork Chops

1 Tablespoon Olive Oil

Olive Oil

Parmesan

1/2 Cup Parmesan Cheese

Cranberry Sauce

1 Can Whole Berry Cranberry Sauce

Salt & Pepper

Orange Juice

1/4 Cup Orange Juice

CHOPPED ONIONS

1 Cup Frozen Chopped Onions

Preheat oven to 400°.
Put on rubber gloves.
Place pork chops
in baking dish.

Sprinkle pork chops with
salt and pepper.

Open can of cranberry
sauce.

Spoon sauce around the pork chops.

Pour orange juice onto
cranberry sauce.

Place dish into oven.
Set timer for 15 minutes.

Place olive oil into saucepan.
Turn heat to medium.

When pan is hot, add
the onions and stir to cook.
(About 3 minutes)

Add the spinach, Stir until wilted.
(About 3 minutes)

Sprinkle with salt and pepper.

Add parmesan cheese.

Mix well.

Remove pan from oven.
And serve.

CHICKEN STEW
With Mixed Vegetables Medley

Knife

Measuring Cup

Measuring Spoons

Large Sauce Pan

Mixing Spoon

4 Cups Chicken Broth

2 Chicken Breasts

1 Cup Milk

1 teaspoon Corn Starch

2 Cups Frozen Mixed Vegetables

1 teaspoon Dry Thyme

CHEF LAURIE TIP | "You may use pre cooked chicken or leftover Turkey from Thanksgiving instead of the raw chicken breasts."

In a large saucepan,
add the chicken broth...

and 2 chicken breasts.
Turn on stove to high.

Bring to a boil.
Set heat to medium.
Let chicken simmer. Set timer
for 10 minutes

Carefully remove chicken.
Place onto cutting board.

Add frozen vegetables...

and thyme.

Mix corn starch
into milk.

Pour into pot

Stir until mixture begins
to thicken.

Cut chicken into medium
size pieces.

Stir and serve.

TURKEY MEATBALLS

With Spinach and Shredded Carrot Salad

Cookie Sheet

Tongs

Rubber Gloves

Parchment Paper

Spoon

Large Mixing Bowl

1 Tablespoon Italian Seasoning

Shredded Carrots

1 Cup of Shredded Carrots

1/2 Cup Parmesan Cheese

1 Egg

1/2 Cup Bread Crumbs

1/4 Cup Low Fat Salad Dressing

1/2 Pound Ground Turkey

3 Cups Baby Spinach

1/2 Cup Marinara Sauce

1/4 Cup Ketchup

1 Cup of Chopped Onions

Salt & Pepper

CHEF LAURIE TIP | " Press the meatball mix into a bread pan and bake for 45 minutes at 350° to make a meatloaf. "

Preheat Oven to 450°.

In a large mixing bowl add
Turkey
Onions
Ketchup
Egg
Parmesan
Bread Crumbs
Salt and Pepper
Italian Seasoning

Line a cookie sheet with parchment paper.

Put on rubber gloves.

Mix together well (for about 1 min) using your hands.

Scoop some turkey into your palm.

In a circular motion...

roll turkey into balls.

Place balls of turkey onto cookie sheet.

Spoon marinara onto balls of turkey.

Place into oven. Set Timer for 12 minutes.

In a mixing bowl, add spinach, shredded carrots...

and salad dressing.

Toss to coat. Remove from oven, and serve.

BLACK BEAN STEW
With Blue Chips And Cucumber Wedges

Can
Opener

Large Sauce Pan

Pot Lid

Measuring
Spoons

Measuring
Cup

Cucumber

1 Can
14 Oz
Diced
Tomatoes

1 Can Black
Beans 14 Oz

Chili
Powder

1 Can
Chile Peppers 3 oz

1 Cup Chopped
Frozen Onions

Blue Corn Chips

1 Cup Celery

Cumin Spice

CHEF LAURIE TIP | " Eat more beans ! Beans are power foods; they are loaded with fiber, protein and antioxidants. "

Dice celery into small pieces.

Open all three cans.

In a large saucepan, place
the celery...

Tomatoes...

Black Beans...

Chopped onions...

and chilies

1 Tablespoon chili powder.
1 teaspoon of cumin.

Turn heat to medium high.

Place lid on pot.
Set timer and
simmer for 15 minutes.

Slice cucumbers into wedges
and serve.

PECAN CRUSTED CHICKEN
With Roasted Red Potatoes And Parmesan Zucchini

Cookie Sheet

Parchment Paper

Food Processor

Rubber Gloves

Tongs

Knife

2 (4 oz) Boneless Chicken Breasts

1 Zucchini

1/2 Cup Pecans

1/2 Pound Small Red Potatoes

Salt and Pepper

1 Cup of Multi-Grain Flakes

1/4 Cup Parmesan Cheese

1/2 Cup Dijon Mustard

" If you don't have a food processor, crush the pecans and cereal in a ziptop bag with a rolling pin. "

PreHeat oven to 450°.
Line a cookie sheet
with parchment paper.

In a small food processor,
add the pecans
and multi-grain flakes.

Pulse until finely chopped.

On a flat surface, lay a sheet
of parchment paper. Place ground
contents of mini-chopper
onto sheet.

Put on rubber gloves.
On another sheet of parchment,
coat each piece of chicken
with dijon mustard on both sides.

Dredge mustard -coated
chicken into cereal mixture.

Place onto cookie sheet.

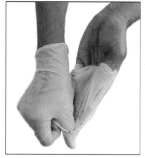
Carefully remove
rubber gloves.

Place gloves onto used sheet
of parchment paper.
Pick up sheet and throw away.

Carefully slice potatoes in half.
Place on paper plate

Microwave on high power for
3 minutes. Place potatoes
next to chicken on cookie sheet.

Slice zucchini into circles.
Place onto cookie sheet.

Spray zucchini, potatoes, and chicken
with olive oil.
Sprinkle with salt and pepper.
Lightly sprinkle zucchini with parmesan.

Place cookie sheet into oven.
Set timer for 13 minutes.
(Chicken will feel firm to the touch.)
Plate and serve.

BEEF STIR FRY
With Teriyaki Vegetables And Brown Rice

Measuring Spoons

Measuring Cup

Bowl

Mixing Spoon

Tongs

Paper Plate

Large Skillet or Wok

2 Cups Vegetable Broth

1/2 Pound Raw Pre-Sliced Lean Beef

1/2 Cup Teriyaki Sauce

2 Tablespoons Olive Oil

12 oz Bag of Frozen Asian Vegetables 12 oz

1 teaspoon Corn Starch

2 Cups Instant Brown Rice

In a medium size ceramic bowl, add the vegetable broth...

and brown rice.

Cover with paper plate and microwave on high for 8 Minutes.

Add corn starch to teriyaki.

Heat a large skillet or wok, until hot but not smoking. Sprinkle olive oil into pan.

Add beef in one layer. Let brown on one side about one minute.

Add bag of vegetables.

Toss in pan with beef.

Pour mixture into pan. Toss to coat. And serve over brown rice.

FISH STICKS

With Corn On The Cob And Asian Cole Slaw

Measuring Cup

Parchment Paper

Rubber Gloves

Knife

Cookie Sheet

Mixing Bowl

2 Ears of Corn

1/2 Pound White Fish (Grouper) (or Bass)

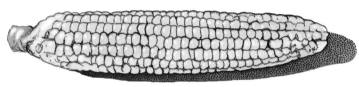

1/2 Cup Parmesan Cheese

Salt & Pepper

1/2 Cup Teriyaki Sauce

1 Bag of Broccoli Slaw

1/2 Cups Panko Bread Crumbs

1/2 Cup Dijon Mustard

1 Tablespoon Olive Oil

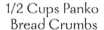

CHEF LAURIE TIP

" Panko is a Japanese style of bread crumbs found in the Asian section of most supermarkets. "

Preheat oven to 450°
Put on rubber gloves.
Carefully slice fish into strips.

Place fish onto parchment paper.
Cover with mustard.

Smear mustard over strips.

On another piece of parchment,
pour the parmesan
and bread crumbs.

Mix together with hands.

Lay parchment paper on a cookie sheet.
Cover fish in mixture.
Place onto sheet.

Place into oven.
Set timer for 12 minutes

Place corn on the corner of a
piece of parchment paper.

Drizzle corn with olive oil.
Sprinkle with salt and pepper..

Fold parchment over corn
and roll up.

Place into microwave for
2 minutes.

Pour desired amount of
coleslaw into mixing bowl.

Pour teriyaki into bowl.
Remove fish from oven.
And Serve.

CHICKEN PARMESAN

With Vegetable Fettucini

Cookie Sheet

Rubber Gloves

Measuring Cup

Oven Mitt

Measuring Spoons

Peeler

Ziptop Bag

Mixing Bowl

Carrot

Zucchini

Salt & Pepper

1 Cup Parmesan Cheese

2 Boneless Chicken Breasts (4 oz each)

1 teaspoon Olive Oil

Squash

1/2 Cup Marinara Sauce

1/4 Cup Panko Bread Crumbs

1 teaspoon Oregano

1/2 Cup Cheese Blend

CHEF LAURIE TIP

" You can add the peeled vegetables to any kind of cooked spaghetti, for a colorful and healthy twist."

Preheat oven to 450°.
In a large mixing bowl, peel a
carrot, zucchini and squash.

Lightly spray with
olive oil.

Add salt and pepper.
Cover with paper plate.

Place in microwave on
high for 2 minutes.

Put on rubber gloves.
Drizzle chicken with
olive oil.

In a ziptop bag,
add Parmesan cheese...

and oregano.

Place chicken breasts
into bag.

Mix all the ingredients
until chicken is
completely covered.

Place into oven.
Set timer for 10 minutes.

Cover chicken in marinara
sauce...

And cheese.

Place into oven
for 5 minutes.

Remove from oven.

ITALIAN PASTA
With Chicken Sausage, Tomatoes, And Peppers

Knife

Measuring Cup

Cutting Board

Measuring Spoons

Mixing Spoon

Pot Lid

Large Sauce Pan

1 teaspoon Basil

1 Cup Penne Pasta

1 Can of Tomatoes (14 Oz)

1 teaspoon Olive Oil

Salt and Pepper

2 Cups Frozen Pepper & Onion Blend

12 oz Cooked Chicken Sausage

CHEF LAURIE TIP | "You can add some diced mozzarella cheese and some chopped fresh basil just before serving."

Put on rubber gloves.
Cut sausage into circles.

Heat a large sauce pan until hot,
but not smoking.
Spray pan with olive oil.

In hot pan, add sausage...

frozen onion / pepper
blend, Tomatoes...

penne pasta...

1 cup water...

and basil.
Stir to combine.

Bring to a boil.
Cover pot with lid,
turn heat to low.

Set timer for 20 minutes.
Stir occasionally.
Add salt and pepper to taste.
And serve with whole wheat roll.
(optional)

BAKED COD

With Tomatoes, Parmesan Orzo, And Sweet Peas

Cookie Sheet

Mixing Bowl

Can Opener

Measuring Cup

Parchment Paper

Measuring Spoons

Paper Plate

1/2 Cup Diced Tomatoes

2 Cod Filets 4 to 6 oz

1/2 Cup Parmesan

1 Teaspoon Italian Seasoning

Salt & Pepper

1/4 Cup Bread Crumbs

2 + 1/2 Cups Chicken Broth

1/2 Cup Wheat Orzo Pasta

1 Cup of Frozen Peas

Preheat oven to 450°.
Line a cookie sheet
with parchment paper.

Place cod filets onto paper.
Sprinkle with salt and pepper.

Cover with tomatoes.
Add italian seasoning...

and bread crumbs.

Place into oven
Set Timer for 12 minutes.

In a mixing bowl, add the
chicken broth
and orzo pasta.

Cover with paper plate.
Place into microwave on high
for 10 minutes.

Remove from oven.
Add peas...

and Parmesan cheese.
Mix together.

Remove sheet from oven.
And serve.

PASTA PRIMAVERA

With Cheesy Pasta And Mixed Vegetables

Measuring Spoons

Measuring Cup

Pasta Pot (with strainer)

Wooden Spoon

Dish Towel

Whisk

Oven Mitt

Mixing Bowl

2 Eggs

1 Cup Parmesan

1 Tablespoon Salt

Whole Wheat Rotini

2 Cups Rotini Pasta

1 teaspoon Onion Powder

LOWFAT MILK

1/2 Cup Low Fat Milk

Frozen Vegetable Mix

1 Bag Frozen Vegetables 12 oz

CHEF LAURIE TIP

" Don't worry about the eggs, the heat of the pasta cooks them in the mixing bowl. "

Place pot and strainer onto stove.
Add 6 cups of water
and 1 Tablespoon of salt.
Turn heat to high.

Bring water to a boil.

Add Pasta.
Set timer for 10 minutes.

Stir occasionally.

Crack two eggs into mixing bowl.

Add milk...

onion powder...

and parmesan cheese.

Pour bag of vegetables into pot
for 2 minutes.

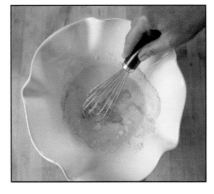

Use the whisk to stir the sauce.

Remove strainer and place onto towel
to drain.

Pour pasta into mixing bowl.
Stir and serve.

CHICKEN FINGERS
With Apple Dijon Sauce And Cheesy Broccoli

Cookie Sheet

Measuring Cup

Parchment Paper

Knife

Ziptop Bag

Mixing Bowl

Measuring Spoons

Rubber Gloves

1 Head of Broccoli

1 Package Chicken Tenders 12 oz

1/4 Cup Panko Bread Crumbs

1/4 Cup Apple Sauce

1/4 Cup Apple Juice Concentrate

1 Tablespoon Olive Oil

1/2 Cup Dijon Mustard

1 Cup Italian Cheese Blend

1 Cup Parmesan Cheese

" Make extra chicken fingers and have them the next day on a salad for lunch. "

Preheat oven to 450 °
Put on rubber gloves.
Inside a ziptop bag add
parmesan and bread crumbs.

Lay a piece of parchment.
Coat chicken with
olive oil.

Dredge all of the chicken.

Place chicken into ziptop bag.

Seal bag and shake until
all chicken is coated.

On a cookie sheet, place a
piece of parchment paper
and then the chicken.

Carefully cut broccoli into
bite-size pieces.
(Discard unused stalk.)

Lightly spray broccoli and
chicken with olive oil.

Bake for 10 minutes until
light brown and crispy.

In a small bowl,
add apple juice
concentrate...

Apple Sauce...

and dijon mustard.

Remove pan from
oven.

Sprinkle cheese over broccoli
and serve.

SALMON TERIYAKI

With Thai Noodles And Snow Peas

Measuring Cup

Pasta Strainer

Measuring Spoons

Mixing Bowl

Cookie Sheet

Rolling Pin

Parchment Paper

Dish Towel

Ziptop Bag

Oven Mitts

Pasta Pot

Two 5 oz Salmon Filets

1/2 Cup Cilantro

2 Tablespoons Teriyaki Sauce

Olive Oil

1/4 Cup Peanuts

1 Cup Snap Peas

8 oz Whole Wheat Pasta

" If your not used to whole wheat pasta try making the dish with half whole wheat and half white pasta. "

Preheat oven to 450°.
In a large saucepan,
add 8 cups of water.
Turn heat to high. Bring to boil.

Line a cookie sheet with
parchment paper.
Place salmon onto sheet.

Spoon teriyaki sauce onto salmon
(about 1 Tablespoon each).

Lay snap peas next to salmon.
Lightly spray with
olive oil.

Sprinkle with salt and pepper.

Place into oven
Set timer for 10 minutes.

Place pasta into boiling water.

Put peanuts into ziptop bag.

Using a rolling pin
(or Wine Bottle)
crush peanuts.

Scoop pasta from pot and strain.

Place pasta onto kitchen towel...

then into mixing bowl.
Add teriyaki sauce...

peanuts...

and cilantro leaves,
Mix together.

Remove sheet from oven,
And serve.

Chef Laurie Erickson is a sought-after wellness cuisine consultant to spas and resorts around the country. During her three-year collaboration with the Sea Island Company, she served as Wellness Chef, developing healthy cooking classes as well as wellness-cuisine menu options for Sea Island, Georgia's Five-Star Resort and Spa. Prior to her tenure at Sea Island, Chef Laurie served as both a pastry and demonstration chef during her six years on the culinary team at the famed *Canyon Ranch Resort and Spa* in Lenox, Massachusetts.

Her cooking classes and demonstrations have changed the lives of many, with practical, simple and economical ways to prepare nourishing meals. Chef Laurie has inspired and mentored several students from the Culinary Institute of America, Johnson and Wales Academy and New England Culinary School.

Her professional insights and recipes have appeared in *Family Circle Magazine, Spa Magazine, People Magazine's Your Diet, Best Life Magazine, Men's Health, The Boston Globe, Forbes Life and Restaurant News*. She has been the featured chef on the *Travel Channel's Epicurious* cooking

show, PBS TV's On the Menu, and on the Tennis Channel. Additionally, Chef Laurie has contributed recipes and cooking tips for *The Canyon Ranch Cooks* cookbook and The New York Times top-selling book, *Ultra Metabolism*. Chef Laurie is a culinary educator, certified fitness instructor and certified sports nutritionist. You can view Chef Laurie in action by watching her cooking videos on her website www.ChefLaurie.com and on YouTube.

She is currently working on her follow-up book in the CHEF*ʙʏ*STEP® series, "Cooking For The Bachelor".

Artist Jake Morrill is a freelance illustrator from Great Barrington, Massachusetts. A recent honors graduate of the University of Hartford, Hartford Art School, Jake majored in Illustration. While at school he adored the mentorship he received, studying under master professors Dennis Nolan, Bill Thomson, and Doug Anderson. The challenges of his strict education were stepping stones in the development of his artistic abilities.

Since then, Jake's work has been featured in publications from the *Wall Street Journal* to the *Society of Illustrators Los Angeles* and prominently displayed in galleries throughout New England *(Norman Rockwell Museum, Joseloff Gallery)*.

Preferring traditional techniques, his paintings are executed with various mediums (acrylic, color pencil, pen and ink) with an uncompromising amount of detail. Aside from his illustrations, Jake has found

great success as a portrait artist, executing numerous commissions this past year. You can view Jake's work at www.Morrillustrations.com.

He is currently working on the follow-up book in the CHEF by STEP® series, "Cooking For The Bachelor ".